P O I N T
T H E
F I N G E R

Also by Duncan Forbes

August Autumn (Secker and Warburg, 1984)
Public and Confidential (Enitharmon, 1989)
Taking Liberties (Enitharmon, 1993)

POINT THE FINGER

Duncan Forbes

The Bodley Head
LONDON

1 3 5 7 9 10 8 6 4 2

Copyright © Duncan Forbes 1994

Duncan Forbes has asserted his rights under the Copyright, Designs
and Patents Act 1988 to be identified as the author of this work

First published in the United Kingdom 1994
by The Bodley Head Children's Books
Random House, 20 Vauxhall Bridge Road, London SW1V 2SA

Random House Australia (Pty) Limited
20 Alfred Street, Milsons Point, Sydney,
New South Wales, 2061, Australia

Random House New Zealand Limited
18 Poland Road, Glenfield,
Auckland 10, New Zealand

Random House South Africa (Pty) Limited
PO Box 337, Bergvlei 2012, South Africa

Random House UK Limited Reg. No. 954009

A CIP catalogue record for this book is available from the
British Library

ISBN 0 370 318 161

Phototypeset by Intype, London
Printed in Great Britain by Mackays of Chatham Plc, Chatham, Kent

CONTENTS

A LETTER FROM THE AUTHOR

People sometimes ask me where I find the ideas for poems and I can honestly reply that the sources seem to vary as much as the poems themselves. They can be prompted by such different sights as a full moon or a scarlet Ford Sierra, aggressively driven. They can also be provoked by a phrase or a few words rattling around in the head or scribbled on a scrap of paper ('Lone Ranger says to Tonto, / "Do you speak Esperanto?" '). A poem may be written in response to an unexpected Christmas present ('Not Tested On Animals'), journeys on the London Underground ('In The Underworld') or a visit to Land's End ('Pen-Von-Las') but it may be about ideas or emotions as well.

I hope that some of the poems included in the collection express my stronger and deeper feelings over such shared concerns and confidences as love, death, anger, fear. Other poems are more public and outspoken statements in response to various issues. Some of the verses have a sense of humour and are often lighter in tone: these include verbal fun and games like 'Blowing My Gaffe' and such satirical squibs as 'Moggie Thatcher' and 'Monosodium Glutamate'. A few of the poems included here, like 'Tomorrow Never' and 'Why Bare Your Body?' are song lyrics waiting for music.

After the event, it is not always easy to remember exactly what went into the writing of a poem such as 'Paper Utopia' or 'Recension Day' but what may be more important now is what readers can gain from the individual poems: thoughts, ideas, feelings, pleasures, questions, images, insights and mysteries which can become part of their own experience.

I started reading and writing poems myself when I was

at school and gradually became fascinated by the challenge of putting thoughts and feelings into words and patterns. Despite what some readers may think, poems are often, in my experience, the result of effort, thought and hard work, however natural or casual they may seem or are made to seem. A few poems emerge quickly for me and with relatively little polishing, but many more are the result of application over days, weeks, months and sometimes even years.

The poems chosen for *Point The Finger* were written over a number of years and not specifically for younger readers. I hope nevertheless that readers of all ages will find something to interest them in this collection. It begins with a look at 'Tribal England' and ends, after various glances at human and natural worlds, with a more searching gaze at the self.

In my view, poetry offers one of the few and best ways we have of sharing our thoughts and feelings with other people. It can also help us to understand our own natures and the world in which we find ourselves.

Duncan Forbes

CAUSE AND EFFECT

Because I am tone-dumb,
Because I cannot sing
Or descant like a bird
On all or everything,
I sometimes think I have done
The next best human thing,
As if arranging words
For the inner ear to hum
Could intimate or bring
Insight into the world,
Hope of a life to come.

TRIBAL
ENGLAND

Take a look at tribal England,
Enter the human zoo,
And look at the lesser-spotted punk
With nothing better to do
Than kick his heels on the bottle bank,
A Mohican cockatoo.

And take the ring-necked vicar next
In his clerical grey,
With his dry sherry eye, old-fashioned clothes,
His biblical text
And his Anglican pigeon toes.

Bald old badger, allotment man,
Keen on his home-grown greens
Is gardening in a cardigan
Bald at each elbow too
As he builds a bamboo wigwam for
His precious runner beans.

See the prat in a cravat,
The zombie in a crombie,
The big fat berk in the off-white Merc
And the chic clique in the back,
The Kevins and Sharons, Fionas and Ruperts,
The rich, the kitsch, the mad, the sad,
The chip-shop queue and the Henley crew
In tribal England's human zoo
And what does that make of me or you?

STORY OF MY LIFE

Trying to free
like a good Hindu
a bumble bee
from the garden shed
I drove it into
a spider's web,
alas, instead.

There trussed and trapped,
a stumbling thing,
it buzzed and flapped,
from angry bull
with grey-haired wing
to irritable
fungus ball.

I flicked it outside
on the tip of a trowel
into the weeds
of a flowerbed
to disentangle
self from web
or try to try to try till dead.

SHELTERED UPBRINGING

Hydrangeas test the soil's acidity.
The mirror triptychs in the bedroom windows
Collect the light in narcissistic pools.
Safe in their Wellingtons and windcheaters
Peter and Jane are helping Daddy garden.
He clips the privet and they feed the bonfire.
Soon they will plant potatoes in its embers
And eat them, hard and gritty, after tea.
At dusk they listen to their bedtime story:
Henry The Green Engine who was immured
For disobedience like Antigone.

BUTTERFLY
COLLECTION

My shadow sidled next to me on tiptoe,
While one Red Admiral spread embroidered
   wings,
Its hair-spring tongue unspiralling to tipple
Scented liqueurs. Robed for investiture,
In doctoral red, white, black and blue, it
   sunbathed,
Hingeing upon its whiskered fuselage
Wings deckle-edged as pencil sharpener
   shavings.
Slowly I wiped my hands against my shorts,
Triggered my thumbs and cupped my fingers
   airtight,
Then waited for the butterfly to fold.
With a sudden snarl of bees and whiff of buddleia,
A tickle clattered in the dark I held.

Indoors was cool and twilit as a larder.
The glass gas-chamber of my screw-top jar
Stank of ammonia drunk by blotting paper.
Closed on the lid, the butterfly at first
Hung passive like a flake of blackened leaf-
   mould.
A wingtip shivered. Repulsively
Its nose-haired abdomen inflated, writhing.
It dropped, capsized, kicked filaments of leg.
Wings flapped as if on fire, but fanned an ember

Which hovered, hopped and scuttled round the
   jar.
My breathing pivoted its hand-held deadness,
Till at its wings' clenched colour plates I tugged.
Dusty pigment marked my fingers guilty.
I fractured its dihedral, just to feel
The smudged transparencies that glazed its
   wingspan.
Then judging the specimen as not for show,
I dropped dismantled bits into a matchbox.
Yet, shut in the dark myself, I couldn't sleep,
But breathed the stuffy air beneath the blankets,
And cowering there in dread of it I prayed
That when it found me the avenging angel
Would smother first whom it would mutilate.

SISTER

Though neither of us ever stood
As straight as mother wished we would,
I stood up straight for, but I lost,
The brother-sister back to backs
Which mother refereed with books
And which I always hoped you'd lose,
You six-foot-tall hypotenuse.

Height was an issue less alive
When I was six and you were five,
Yet at a fancy dress parade,
Crawling behind you on all fours
I wished my mask had proper jaws
Because my wolf was not as good
As you, you smug Red Riding Hood.

And even when we went to school
We learnt no equalizing rule,
Since your best subject was my worst
And you sat in and did for fun
The Maths that I was coached to learn.
So what made you turn Classicist,
Except that I had started first?

But then you won, to my disgrace,
The year I gained an Oxford place,
Your exhibition to St Anne's.
Though I resented you there more
After I'd found you in my room
Getting much further with a man
Than I'd got girls on that divan.

When people asked if we were twins
I matched our sallow, greasy skins,
Brown hair, brown eyes and lanky stance,
But now I wonder if they meant
Some symmetry of temperament,
Caused not so much by common genes
As competition in our teens.

So now I've got, while you have none,
A younger sister for my son,
I hope that they'll be different,
But let's hope, if they do compete,
They're sooner to admit defeat
Than both their father and their aunt,
Who haven't done so, till they can't.

ANOTHER COUNTRY

Sketched by a thirsty watercolourist,
Kids on hind legs, miniature black goats,
Begged an olive for its greenest shoots.
Hens pecked at their own shadows in the dust.
And a girl came, as if from a taverna,
Holding a perfumed, sugar-powdered cake
And a glittering beaker of stone-cooled retsina.
The young man thanked her, drank and ate.
Her questions were incomprehensible,
So on his pad he wrote in Attic Greek
With a Made in England 2B Venus pencil:
γραφω ἀλλα οὐ φημι – I write but do not speak –
And her amazement at the oracle
Flattered his manhood like the alcohol.

WATERSHED

The Bow River. Bow River.
Three men in his anecdote,
One with an artificial leg,
Were heading for rapids in a boat
On the Bow River. Or wherever.
Vague memories of lake and muskeg
In the Arctic Watershed
Looked for a Bow to rediscover.
Is that in Canada? I said.

Rocky Mountains. Banff, Alberta.
I know it, yes, and Lake Louise.
A girl, the current and a canoe
Are moving with me past dark trees
Once more into the unlived future
Fifteen or sixteen summers ago
One summer evening, almost night,
On cold coppery-green melt-water
Which I thought I would never forget.

UNCERTAINTY

Graves of husbands, wives and lovers,
Like the churchyard manhole covers,
Proudly bear their maker's name,
But they're rotting all the same
When the earth the vicar blessed
And the turves have detumesced.

Whether I or you die first —
Can't think which I've most rehearsed —
Senseless fossil pollen grains
Will date our animal remains
To the first years grass grew flowers
Over either grave of ours.

But the knowledge I shall die
Cannot also tell me why,
Nor can all there ever is,
Nor all brief posterities
From Pre-Cambrian year dot
Till the universe is not.

THE WAY THINGS ARE

The coffee shivers in concentric rings
And as the quayside seems to float inland
I walk on deck for sea air and to watch
Weymouth become a postcard of itself,
Dorset a breakwater, the coastline cloud,
Our wake a ragged motorway of foam,
Where both a pigeon and a cabbage white
Are following the Red Ensign out to sea.

Back in the cafeteria-lounge, the youth
In Megadeth T-shirt and blue neckerchief,
The skull-and-crossbones buckle on his belt,
And reading Isaac Asimov is my son.
The girl with hiccups, sipping Diet Pepsi
And wearing a pink T-shirt, is my daughter.
Black cut-off jeans, blue watch-strap, pony-tail,
She's playing Guns 'N' Roses on a Walkman.

Rock muzak, rucksacks, Keep This Ship Tidy
   Bins,
Bermuda shorts, a Michael Jackson T-shirt,
A girl with earrings eating custard creams,
The mood is holiday and duty-free.
My wife is reading a Virago novel,
The Way Things Are by E. M. Delafield.
She's chewing Orbit sugar-free chewing gum
But says she'd love 200 cigarettes.

Safety announcements in both French and
    English
Have spoken of emergency procedures,
Life-jackets, muster-stations, crew and drill,
A series of short blasts upon the whistle,
While I imagine what would happen if,
And in the daydream minutes before drowning
I play the hero and apologist
For love so long denied and ill-expressed.

RECENSION DAY

Unburn the boat, rebuild the bridge,
Reconsecrate the sacrilege,
Unspill the milk, decry the tears,
Turn back the clock, relive the years,
Replace the smoke inside the fire,
Unite fulfilment with desire,
Undo the done, gainsay the said,
Revitalize the buried dead,
Revoke the penalty and clause,
Reconstitute unwritten laws,
Repair the heart, untie the tongue,
Change faithless old to hopeful young,
Inure the body to disease
And help me to forget you please.

PLEASURE

The only problem being where to begin
With such a bosomy buttocky physique:
To kiss, to nibble, bite or stroke the skin
Of downy suntan like a baby's cheek?

Fructified sunlight for pale northern flesh
To sink its apple-cleaned incisors in
Then wipe the fruit juice dripping from the chin.
The peach, *la pesca*, feminine, *la pêche*.

And taste the Mediterranean vitamin
Of one imported Common Market peach
More luscious than the slices in a tin,
Fresh peaches, blushing ripe and ten pence
   each.

Even the peach-stone in the roof of the mouth
Would seem to fit the palate like a plate
Until the bow-point of the rowing boat
Needles the skin between the two front teeth.

Then suck the red meat from the wrinkled bone
Held to the life- and love-lines of the hand,
And dream how the kernel of this wooden brain,
If it were buried in its native land,
Could make a peach tree come to life again.

HOT WATER

The best bit of it, though, is getting in.
Hot water. Godliness. And naked skin.
So could this be the ultimate solution,
A dissolute dissolving in sensation,
A melting of both duty and desire
To a pure pleasure in the temperature?
The coloured abstracts and the full-length nude
Self-portrait, blameless in its self-regard,
The engine-room blood-noises of the brain
Relaxing underneath the water-line
Feel amniotic if not infinite.
Even the mini-whirlwind in the whirlpool
Gyrating at so many revs per minute
Repeats the planet's centripetal pull.

BOIS JOLY

Dog barking
on a distant farm,
sun setting,
half a risen moon,
a combine harvester's
red drone,
stubble smell,
smell of corn.

Swifts wheel above
a sunflower field,
the buds turned west,
flowers east,
where I stand like
a pantheist,
blessing sunlight,
being blessed.

12th July
'89,
Bois Joly
was the hamlet's name.
Someone else
some other time
had felt like me
if not the same.

Orange peel in the snow,
orange or satsuma.
The boy on the bicycle,
armband on each arm
orange against the ice
and each a lucky charm,
is irreplaceable.
What could reproduce
the boyish sense of humour
and his particular smile,
winter spring and summer?

DANDELION

The sun is a dandelion flower,
The moon a dandelion clock
And we who have been here an hour
Compared to Pre-Cambrian rock
And can call a flower a weed
Seem to have no more power
Than any airborne seed.

CHERRY BLOSSOM BLACK

Kneeling like some strange four-footed beast
And cleaning my unfashionable shoes,
By which I mean elastic-sided boots,
On an old newspaper's forgotten news,
I dab the brush into the tin and try
Not to get any blacking on my suit,
Dark socks, white shirt cuffs, or the borrowed tie
As matt black as the polish on the boot.

The formal neck- and footwear of male grief
Serve as disguises for the funeral.
The tin and tin-lid, paper and still life
Are both a memory and memorial:
The sounds of shoeshine and the polish smell,
The putter-onner and the taker-off.

THE TOUCH

The Amphitheatre Entrance, Covent Garden.
Asked there for twopence for a cup of tea
The question smelt so methylated that
I both refused him change to buy his drink
And then the handshake which he offered me.
Though that was unforgivable, I think,
He shook his head and gave my arm a pat,
Able uncomprehendingly to pardon.

Later, on stage in a Verona square,
In came a dancer with a gammy leg,
In rags, on crutches, carrying a bowl
Among the corps de ballet idling there,
And though I knew that it was just a role,
I begged that he, though paid to, wouldn't beg.

PAPER
UTOPIA

This is an equal opportunities statement.
Although it already has charitable status
And the rates on any building in which it is read
Are automatically zero-rated for a decade,
It seeks publicity no more than a test-tube
   foetus.

The recycled paper on which it is printed
Has been impregnated with potent microdots
Which when chewed are guaranteed to provide
A tasty meal of over 4000 calories
With vitamins A to E for a family of four.

Scrumpled, it's a briquette of smokeless fuel
Which yields over three slow-burning
   megawatts.
The bottom left corner contains enough
   oestrogen
To be used as a fail-safe oral contraceptive.
Catholics may use it as a communion wafer.

It is all part of the ecumenical movement
And has been recognized by no less than the
   Pope,
The Kremlin, the White House and the EEC.
It has been approved by the silent majority,
And endorsed by such vocal minorities as

Christian Aid, the Basque Separatists
And the Variety Club of Great Britain, among
  many others.
It will end all wars, murder and masturbation.
It will annihilate disease and poverty.
It will eliminate all famines and droughts.

Like the Queen and her God of whose Anglican
  Church she is nominal head,
This document is officially of no political
  persuasion
And it does not carry any legal tender,
Though it may be the paper money of the future.
Anyone copying it by whatever means

Will be personally thanked. The film rights are
  free.
Correctly folded, it makes an origami Concorde,
Being a small but British contribution
To the freedom-fighters fighting for freedom
From oppression, pollution and over-population.

The letters in it are symbols of human
  endeavour,
And the white space around it stands for
  Antarctica,
The largest relatively unspoilt wilderness
On the planet misnamed Earth
Which should have been Ocean.

ULEY HOUSE

The flattened molehills stepping-stone the lawn
Towards fresh soil-heaps near the Judas tree.
Pink clematis flowers embrace a rusty cypress.
The creaking wingbeats of a wood pigeon
Applaud its exit from a copper beech
Into a sky of Pentecostal light
On a jasmine, bluebell, lilac-scented evening.
Rooks argue and a dog barks at a gunshot.
Among full moons of dandelion clocks
Heifers are tearing grasses in the sunset.
It's country life as *Country Life* would have it
And I'm so passive or dispassionate
I hear a desiccated holly leaf
Detach itself and fall through leaves to earth.

IN THE UNDERWORLD

Clockwatchers stare at advertising space
Where Pornutopia meets with paradise
And promised lands of vines and lingerie
Ransom their happiness at purchase price.

There is a beggar man at Waterloo,
At Piccadilly needles and syringe.
At Oxford Circus a fly-posted booth
Is advertising what the flesh will do.

The poster of a famous opera star
Has pupils made of tooth-marked chewing-gum
Which blinds his eyes and Frankensteins his
    stare.
A smear of curry sauce has smudged him dumb.

With his guitar case for a begging-bowl
A student haunts a subterranean song.
A carborundum spark of stainless steel
Lights up the tunnel like a smoker's lung.

This is both human sewer and London Zoo.
Each mica grain inside its metal stair
Glitters as steely as a distant star.
We are the souls in Purgatorio.

ST FREEDOM

Destitute children
sleep in the doorways
of Tiffany's, Macy's
in sub-zero weather
and, arms over faces
to block out the striplights,
men sleep in a hostel
as big as a hangar,
and an ordinary woman
like Ivy from Brooklyn
can't find an apartment
for herself and three children,
or Martinique Mary,
illegally cooking
and eking a living
on relief from the city,
is raising a family
of girl boy and baby
in a seedy hotel room
in Skid Row, Manhattan,
where mental disturbance
and adult sex movies,
where dope and the pushers,
the raping of children
and murders are normal,
and high unemployment,
population explosion,
the current world crisis,

inflation, recession,
high rents and scarce housing,
high prices, low wages,
as if nothing can stop them,
are blamed for the people
who sleep in the subways
and scavenge in garbage,
take charity handouts
of sandwich or mittens
from volunteer workers
who talk of Charles Dickens
and fear for a future
where no life is sacred,
while millions of dollars
are spent on a statue,
the Statue of Liberty's
world-famous colossus,
restored and refurbished,
saying, 'Give me, oh, give me,
your tired huddled masses,
your poor and your homeless
and I shall ignore them.'

HEATWAVE

1,2,3,4,5,6,7
Butterflies on a buddleia.
The water-skier in the sky
Practises a deadlier
Calligraphy
In a sky-blue . . . call it heaven

Of such innate perfection
It seems ungracious to deny
The vicar-lepidopterist
Who sees in butterfly
And chrysalis
Proof of the resurrection.

CAVIA PORCELLUS

Claw-footed, and timid as a bird
That at last had learnt to feed, afraid,
From the hand that held the vegetable diet
Of carrot and apple, day in, day out,
Or fresh-picked dandelion leaves in season.

Water bottle rattling the grille of her prison,
The sounds of claws on *The Daily Telegraph*,
Smell of sawdust and rodent whiff,
What did they mean to the fidgeting nose?
Did the felt-brown ears enjoy the noise
Of glottal squeaks and high-pitched squeals
In a hungry dialect of vowels?

What did she make of our bicycles?
The short-lived mother-love of girls?
Winter starlight, January frost,
The stifling days of July and August,
And Emmanuel Church clock striking the hours
During her third and fourth guinea-pig years?

What do you make of anything anyway
Lying alone in a garden shed
In a plywood hutch and upside dead?

FLOWER SHOW

Would rose bushes exhibit if they could
Our sexual organs in a vase of blood?

A ROSE REPLIES

No, let it be said,
We plants are well-bred
And the thoughts of roses are pure.
We'd cut off your head
Before you were dead
And grind your bones for manure.

NEWPORT BAY

All stones look semi-precious on the beach,
If not to the fishermen in waterproofs
Or to the scatty Border Collie bitch
Racing below the sedimentary cliffs
Over the yeasty foam into the waves.
A balding man with full-sized bucket and spade
Is digging in the sand for lugworm bait.
One of the anglers, tired of hooking weed,
Catches a fish at last, a bass he says,
Long as his forearm and five pounds in weight,
Then folds the gasping metal of the fish
Into a rubbish sack to suffocate.
Rain smudges the horizon as I watch
A black sack flapping and the tide going out.

LIFE CYCLE

Between a sandbar and a tethered boat
Where river water and sea-currents meet
Under the sand-locked castle on a cliff,
I sit in the lee of a dune and watch
A stripy black and yellow football sock
Of caterpillar clambering up the slope.
Sand avalanches and it starts again,
Its short black legs treadmilling up the hill.
Herb Elliott. Sisyphus. Robert the Bruce.
A larva searching for its only food
Until I scoop it up, its head still peering,
And throw it over my shoulder like spilt salt,
Wishing it ragwort, more than it can eat,
And the wings next summer of a cinnabar moth.

MONEY, MONEY

The money spider that's abseiling
like a shining drop of cider
with a violinist's fingers
from the ceiling by the lampshade
tempts me to philosophize:
may it bring me luck and money;
may I bring it warmth and flies.

O

Sat and watched
full moon at moonrise
totally eclipsed
by a chimney-stack.

Circular moonshine,
linear brickwork:
grandfather clock
time out of mind.

SNAIL ON AN ACANTHUS

Suspended in a slice of air
And looking headfirst down the cliff,

A snail on an acanthus leaf
Searches for things to do or eat.

Its wrinkled footsole licks the edge.
The horns detect no thoroughfare,

So round it turns at snail speed
And helmets through the spiny glade,

All of my squiggles on the page
Mocked by a silver signature.

ANOTHER DYING SWAN?

There was bread on the ice and pigeons feeding
Pink-footed round the thoughts of the swan.
The other, the cob or maybe the pen,
The one with the wing damaged by vandals,
Walked on the ice, black flippers skating.
The trees were freaks, the park Antarctic,
The pond opaque. The two swans usually
Paddled a water-lane free overnight,
But after this heaviest frost of the year
One was jacked up on the ice and the other
Icebound, a pained expression on its profile,
Eye a malevolent, jaundiced bead
In a peevish head of haughty pique,
Until it shivered or seemed to shiver;
And was it a tear that its eyelid squeezed
Glistening down the feathery cheek
And past the carrot-seed of its nostril
To drip from the rim of its mandarin beak?

It drew an inquisitive Sunday crowd
And steaming questions. Were its feet
Trapped under the ice? Was it dying
Of cold or thirst? And did it really
Want to be rescued? Had officialdom been
  called?
The swan made no move to eat the bread
When children vainly shooed it to its feet.
A Scotsman returned with a pickaxe handle,
And his wife, plump in a quilted anorak,
Eyed the municipal red and white lifebelt
As he hacked a path of broken pack-ice
Towards the bird, when the haft suddenly
Slipped from his grasp and vanished under.
How easy it was to disappear!
How difficult to help the helpless creature —
Which having at last had enough of failure
Stood huffily up and shuffled away
Leaving a pool for the other to drink from
And one white feather sailing the surface.

WILDLIFE POSTER

Dressed like a bat for a fancy dress ball,
A SEAGULL flounders in acres of oil.
A HEDGEHOG, flattened by a radial tyre,
Bleeds through its scalp of horrified hair.
Suspected of rabies, a FOX is shot,
And it's Belsen for BADGER inside its set.
A SALMON floating with warts on its face
Lies flat on its back in industrial waste.
A SWALLOWTAIL's mad aerobatic displays
Are caused by the pep in insecticide spray.
SPRUCE is felled for journalist's froth.
SEALS are orphaned, then bludgeoned to
   death.
But a CROW has a live young RABBIT to eat
And starts by pecking its eyeball out.

PEN-VON-LAS

In the telephone wires
Wind is intoning
A warped whale music.
Smoke from coal fires
Frays horizontal.
Gale-force westerlies
Blow out the pilots
In geyser and night-sky.

With spray and a hiss
Water is seething
Around a wet rock
As at its genesis
In the Pre-Cambrian
Igneous ocean.
No wonder Celts called this
The End of the Earth.

SUNSET AND MOONRISE

Feeling less honoured than demeaned
To be supposed susceptible
To setting sun or rising moon,
I try imagining for myself
The tolling of a marker-buoy,
Sunlight on a hoisted sail,
The moonlight painting in the mind
Off Portland Bill or Studland Bay
A liquid moon and molten sun
In watercolours so sublime
They might become the sight of God
Given to visionaries off their guard,
As if there's nothing more to say
Once you have witnessed from the sea
Sunset over Portland Bill,
Moonrise over Studland Bay.

HERON

'Who would choose to be a heron
Wading tiptoe through the shallows,
Staring at the ebbing water,
A daddy-long-legs of a bird
Stabbing minnows for his dinner,
Flapping off on heron's errands,
Anorexic and absurd?'

'Who would choose to be a human,
Glibly, gloomily assuming
What it is to be a heron?
You who cannot even fly
Desecrate my estuary
With your sewage, oil and shipping.
Frankly, I would rather die.'

PRISONER OF CONSCIENCE

Thirteen shiny tins
of John West Pink salmon
have been spot-welded, I think,
onto a curved steel wire
to simulate body and spine
of a sockeye salmon leaping
out of the sculptor's mind
into the leasehold air
of a shrine to art and Mammon.

Fish-head and fish-tail
are burnished aluminium.
The eyes of Indian ink
follow you round the room.
If salmon could speak to salmon,
this creature would be
their crucified Statue of Liberty.
By the millennium
perhaps it will stink.

CUSTOMERS

The sky's in purdah.
Two dead shuttlecocks
perch on a dusty window ledge.
The ropes and nets in the gymnasium
are tied back like girls' hair.
Eleven candidates
are sitting *Use of German*
Indian file between
93 empty chairs
at 94 empty desks.
4.30 on a Friday afternoon.
And how would you express
the following in German?
That's the way to treat customers.
I'd like six strong nails.
A tube of all-purpose adhesive.
The sky's in purdah.
Two dead shuttlecocks.

HOW TO WIN FRIENDS AND INFLUENCE ENEMIES

Notify the notary
Activate the Rotary
Cultivate the coterie
Mystify the pacifists
Pacify the activists
Intimate the enmity
Advertise the amnesty
Ratify the dadaists
Nullify the nihilists
Edify the edifice
Justify injustices
Purify the prurient
Horrify the Puritan
Sanitize insanity
Offer It a cup of tea
Magnify the trivia
Mollify the mafia
Signify the dignitaries
Dignify the signatories
Iconize the human face

Idolize the human race
Ossify the officers
Crucify the Lucifers
Stultify the other ranks
Implicate the lending banks
Massacre the buffalo
Dispossess the Eskimo
Synthesize the sympathy
Improvise a symphony
Demonstrate the Virgin Birth
Microwave the planet Earth.

HIYO SILVER
III

Lone Ranger says to Tonto,
'Do you speak Esperanto?
Because a desperado,
An evil-looking dago,
Is incommunicado
South of San Diego
With a million-dollar cargo
Stolen from Wells Fargo
En route from El Dorado,
'n' I gave my Spanish lexicon
To a hacienda-mender
Who hailed from Texicana,
An alcoholic Mexican
Who wore a red bandanna.'

Says Tonto to Lone Ranger,
'You lead me into danger.
I speak your gringo lingo
And a patchy fake Apache
But no savvy Esperanto
So piss off, *komo sabay*.
And who takes all the glory
For bourgeois law and order
At the end of each week's story?
Not Zorro's little sidekick,
Your obedient factotum.
So give me back my freedom,
My wigwam and my wampum.
I'm heading for the border . . .'

Sheriff and companion
Ride into the canyon.
In Tonto's tawny gullet
They find a silver bullet.

MR MACHO
MACHINATION

Make a conquest, make a killing,
Make a Machiavellian million,
Hi bambino, *ciao amigo*,
Megastar of superego,
Underneath whose white tuxedo
Lurks a psychopath's libido.

All the world's your operation,
Mr Macho Machination
Of the Macho Corporation,
Master of manipulation
(Real name on application),
Mr Macho Machination.

Impress the dumb blondes and the bimbos
With your status and its symbols —
Your multi-gym would rival Rambo's
With its neat machismo gizmos
In the multi-million mansion
Where you hold yourself to ransom.

Mr Macho Machination,
Evangelist of tax evasion,
Master of manipulation,
Alias and allegation,
Diplomat of degradation,
Mr Macho Machination.

Choose a victim, then evict him,
Victory is an addiction.
Life's a game where you're grandmaster,
Courting fortune and disaster.
It's a fact you thrive on fiction:
He played fast but you play faster.

Mr Macho Machination,
Diplomat of degradation,
Doctor of indoctrination,
All the world's your operation,
Beware of any imitation,
Mr Macho Machination.

THANK GOD
IT'S
CHRISTMAS

Every cracker has a motto,
Every motto's truly grim,
The Nativity by Giotto
Comes with love from Joan and Jim.
Suffering the little children
To confide their dreams in him,
Father Christmas in his grotto
Listens to a muzak hymn.

The Pope is singing *Little Donkey*
On the Vatican's new label,
Mr Jones in person is
The archangel Gabriel
In the curate's modern version
Of the story from the Bible
Where a newborn god is breastfed
By a virgin in a stable.

The God of thermal underwear
Is rolling out the Xmas barrel,
Dame Kiri Te Kanawa hails
Mary in a Maori carol,
Ceramic seraphim hosannah
Joseph and the virgin birth,
Santa makes his reindeer canter
Over clouds and down to earth.

On the merry Xmas telly
Terry Wogan's on the blink,
Office bottle-party hearties
Stuff the mind with food and drink
In the central over-heating
Never stop to stop and think
Of the hungry thirsty homeless
In this world of swim or sink.

AUTOMOTIVE MAN

I am a holy terror
In my scarlet Ford Sierra
And I drive as fast as I can.
I rarely use the mirror
In my scarlet Ford Sierra,
I'm antisocial automotive man.

At roundabouts and junctions
My lights all fail to function
And I drive as fast as I can.
I never stop for hikers,
For cyclists or for bikers,
I'm antisocial automotive man.

Whichever way I'm facing
I think I'm motor racing
And I drive as fast as I can.
I come up fast behind you,
Then flash my lights to blind you,
I'm antisocial automotive man.

When I see a woman driver
My mouth fills with saliva
And I drive as fast as I can.
I have to overtake her,
To make her brake or break her,
I'm antisocial automotive man.

The company is paying
For the games that I am playing
And I drive as fast as I can.
I am a holy terror
In my scarlet Ford Sierra,
I'm antisocial automotive man.

My Sierra is a devil
From the mountains to sea level
And I drive as fast as I can.
I'm not a good mechanic
But my motor is satanic,
I'm antisocial automotive man.

EIGHTEEN CHILDREN

Think of all the propaganda
Selling what we do not need,
Think of all the goods that pander
To desire and not to need,
Look at all the bottled water,
Think of all the cattle feed,
Think of all the righteous anger
You expend on what you read.

Then lay the blame and point the finger,
Tell me why if you can say
Eighteen children die of hunger
Every minute, every day.

Think of eighteen living children
In the playground of your head,
Think of names and picture faces,
Hear them laughing one-to-one,
Think of them as nephews, nieces,
As your sister, daughter, son,
Picture them as going thirsty,
Think of them as underfed.

Then lay the blame and point the finger,
Tell me why if you can say
Eighteen children die of hunger
Every minute, every day.

Eighteen children every minute,
If you can't see how it's done,
If you can't imagine children,
Picture your young self as one.
Sixty seconds left to live in,
Dehydrated, underfed,
Twenty seconds left to die in,
Count the blessing when you're dead.

Then lay the blame and point the finger,
Tell me why if you can say
Eighteen children die of hunger
Every minute, every day.

MOGGIE
THATCHER

My name is Moggie Thatcher, I'm a biter and a
  scratcher,
      I'm renowned for landing on my feline feet.
I'm the grocer's puss from Grantham, who
  became the National Anthem,
      And I like expensive cuts of public meat.
Though painted as the brashest tyrannical old
  fascist
      To rule the land without the common
         touch,
I'm proud to think I'm British and both resolute
  and skittish —
      You don't kick Iron Lady in the crutch.

My name is Moggie Thatcher, I'm a biter and a
  scratcher,
      And survival is the nature of the beast,
Working late and with the light on, at the Grand
  Hotel in Brighton,
      I've got another seven lives at least.
My culture is the gin set, the Finchley pearls and
  twinset,
      Britannia reincarnate rules the waves!
Britannia reincarnate in the streets of Friern
  Barnet,
      The unemployed can be employed as
        slaves.

MONOSODIUM GLUTAMATE

My name is Mr Major,
A middle-aged old stager,
Appeaser and assuager,
What else is in *Who's Who*?
No temperament or trauma,
Reliable performer,
What can we say of Norma,
Except she's normal too?

My past has not been wicked,
Nor sexually explicit,
No mud you sling will stick, it
Will come out in the wash.
Dry cleaning — that's the ticket,
The Commons is my wicket,
My passion is Test cricket,
I'm not a toff or posh.

I'm not an academic,
My forte's not polemic,
I represent the Wemmick
In Britain's dreaming spires.
Appealing to blue rinses
With double chins on chintzes,
I hold my own with princes
And the chinless in the shires.

Because all good Conservatives
Are Church and God preservatives
And their ideas derivatives
Of yesterday today,
The God to whom I pray is
Like all that I can say is
A cliché on a dais,
Déclassé, drab and grey.

ZUBR SONG

I am a lonely zubr in a zoo,
Lugubrious and sober is my moo,
I'm a zubr not from Cuba nor Peru,
A zubr not a zebra nor a gnu,
I cannot play the tuba or kazoo.
I'm a European bison
And I've got as much damn licence
To be a European
As any human being being you.

The Zubr name is Russian, don't you know?
We're distant cousins of the buffalo
But Europeans come and bison go
Like Shawnee, Pawnee, Sioux and Navajo —
The zubr stock is also getting low.

I wouldn't mind some roughage now
But not with the giraffe:
I think I need a zubr cow
With whom to share a laugh;
We'd swear the zubr marriage vow
And raise a zubr calf.

All torso, tail and tassel,
I may seem a living fossil
Of hair and horn and muscle,
Bovine and colossal,
But to me there's more than meets the human
 view
And the universe is studied by me too
At Whipsnade University, it's true,
And I've got another name or two for you
Whose ancestors put mine in zubr stew.
I'm a European bison
And I've got as much damn licence
To be a European
As any human being being you.

TOMORROW
NEVER

I like the way you look at me
Across a three-course meal,
I like the way wine works on you
And how it makes me feel.
There's no time like the present
And we've got hours to kill,
The past is obsolescent
And the future never will
So why delay for ever?
Let's spend the night together.
Today is always here: tomorrow never.

That glass of yours looks empty:
Do you need another drink?
Do you want a cup of coffee?
Do you need more time to think?
There's no time like the present,
There's no time like the past,
There's no time like the future
And eternity is vast.
So why delay for ever?
Let's spend the night together.
Today is always here: tomorrow never.

If I'm a man of action,
Then you're a *femme fatale*,
Let's go for satisfaction
And a good time to recall.
There's no time like the present
And time's got us to kill,
The past is obsolescent
And the future never will.
So why delay for ever?
Let's spend the night together.
Today is always here: tomorrow never.

WHY BARE YOUR BODY?

Why pretend you're shallow
When you're really deep?
Why be dishonest
About where you sleep?
Why make a promise
You can never keep?
And why bare your body
If you don't bare your soul?

Why say you want me
When you don't want to know?
Why say you love me
If you never will?
Why say forever
When you mean until?
Oh why bare your body
If you don't bare your soul?

Why talk of passion
If it isn't real?
Why fake compassion
When you fail to feel?
Why say tomorrow
When you mean not at all?
Why say you're sorry
When you're not sorrow-full?

In showrooms of the future
To scrapheaps of the past,
Nothing lasts forever,
Nothing's made to last
And there may be no knowing
If you don't even know:
But why bare your body
If you don't bare your soul?

BACHIANAS BRASILIERAS NO. 5

Salli Terri (soprano)
sings on CBS
an air by Villa-Lobos
arranged for guitar and voice,
and I who know what neither
truth nor beauty is
close my eyes and listen
as if there were nothing else.

HEINZ

The emperor's new clothes
Are another can of worms
Wearing a bowler hat.

The worms are on their toes,
The can is full of beans,
All naked. Fancy that!

DEJECTION ODE

Knickers wet and in a twist,
With myself I am off-pissed.
Up a gum-tree, feeling narked
To have up the wrong tree barked!

POSTCARD

Soaking up the sun in Woking.
Only joking.
Really soaking.
Tent is leaking.
Never spend a week in Woking!

BLURB

Here's a picture of me in a po-faced pose,
A well-groomed self looking down his nose
At all the publicity-conscious prose.

But what if he's hoping that words might matter
Above all the chances to witter and flatter?
Head of dead poet brought in on a platter.

BLOWING MY GAFFE

You could have heard a pin drop
When I'd dropped that brick.
The pause was so pregnant
It started to be sick.

All eyes in the building
Were watching like a hawk's;
Some were out like organ stops,
The rest were out on stalks.

Mouths not gaping watered,
The breath they bated smelt.
Tongues would soon start wagging
Where butter wouldn't melt.

The smell of something brewing
Was worse than in a vat;
Some smelt something fishy,
Others smelt a rat.

Even those on tenterhooks
Were shaken to the core.
Those not shaken rigid
Made beelines for the door.

But did I bat an eyelid?
Did I turn a hair?
Though my heart was in mouth
I beat it out of there.

NOT TESTED ON ANIMALS

Dear Andrew & Barbie, Many thanks.
Moroccan Rhassoul Mud Shampoo
For Hair Type: greasy with dry scalp!
How could you and how did you know?
A Body Shop shampoo which leaves
Moroccan grit grains in the bath
And looks like genuine sham poo.
Oh thank you, thank you, thank you both
And Happy New Hair to you too!

WINE AND CHEESE

Spare me, oh spare me
The kitschery, the bitchery,
The putschery, the butchery,
The hatchet-job obituary,
The stench of the unsavoury
And overcrowded aviary,
The ludic and the ludicrous,
The Judases and Boudiccas,
The hammy and the homily
And all the Royal Family,
The prudery, the rudery,
The lechery, the pseudery,
The mediocre miseries'
Committees on self-pity
And the alcoholic frolics
Of a melancholic colleague
In the arty-farty party
Of karate literati,
To which if you invite me
I will thank you most politely —
And pretend to be delighted
When I haven't been invited.

THE GREY
SQUIRREL

White settlers
trousered Africa
gardened America
Cocacolonized Asia
shop-soiled Australia
oiled Antarctica
footmarked the moon
in the name of Father
Ghost mankind
machine
Amen.

FOCUS

Steady the hand to concentrate the sunbeams.
Remember pinnacles of light on paper,
The tiny smoke signal, then carbon circle,
The brittle hay-blade smoking until felled?

Or in the hands of the less scrupulous
How sunlight could both persecute an insect
Or singe the bare legs of an enemy
And flatten cities into mute surrender?

AND IN THE END?

Hardly have the primeval gases cooled,
Hardly has the volcanic magma boiled
When strange amoebae in the staring water
Die from the massive lack of oxygen.
The leafless conifers decay and fall.
Sea levels rise. The continents dissolve.
Tectonic plates and katabatic winds
Inherit the scorched surface of the earth.
The blood-red eyesore of a hotter sun
Tempers the igneous rocks to brick-kiln heat
In purple daylight full of sediment.
Weird sunsets haemorrhage in the stratosphere,
While rotting seaweed and dead shellfish smells
Linger for fifteen lunar months or more.
The polar ice-caps melt, till all the water
Evaporates in centrifugal fogs
Leaving the seabed as a glomerate
To harden in an airless atmosphere.
Hotplate by day, intensely cold by night,
The planet comes to emulate its moon:
No clouds, no rainfall, season, wind or sound.

Light-years away, in ignorance of this,
The stars are glinting in their dark address.

WHAT NEXT?

Picture a planet
ploughing a furrow
from yesterday
towards tomorrow

Imagine life
and people on it
imagining space
as infinite

Imagine death
and what's beyond it
as both the end
and open-ended

as if the River
Universe
were both forever
and a hearse

and what you've got
is what you have
from the high-chair
to the grave

as if the night
beyond the tomb
were also that
before the womb.

ON A LINE
FROM
CAVAFY

The hunter-gatherers settled into tribes,
Grew seeding grasses and fermented grapes,
Domesticated dogs and outlawed rapes,
Invented money and accepted bribes,
Decided they descended from the apes,
Told nationalistic jokes and published jibes,
Then watched their animal selves on
   videotapes.
Electric typewriters replaced the scribes
But no machine can free me from myself,
The luggage that I carry is the mind,
The mortal envelope is self-addressed
And there's no ship to take me from myself,
To liberate a soul so disinclined
Either to count his blessings or be blessed.